MAKING
MAGIC WINDOWS

Creating Papel Picado/Cut-Paper Art
with CARMEN LOMAS GARZA

CHILDREN'S BOOK PRESS/LIBROS PARA NIÑOS
SAN FRANCISCO, CALIFORNIA

Children's Book Press is grateful to the SBC Foundation whose generous donation has supported the publication of *Making Magic Windows: Creating Papel Picado/Cut-Paper Art with Carmen Lomas Garza.*

Editor: Judith Dunham
Design and Production: Katherine Tillotson

Children's Book Press is a nonprofit publisher of multicultural literature for children, supported in part by grants from the California Arts Council. Write us for a complimentary catalog: Children's Book Press, 246 First Street, Suite 101, San Francisco, CA 94105

Distributed to the book trade through Publishers Group West. Quantity discounts are available through the publisher for educational and nonprofit use.

Library of Congress Cataloging-in-Publication Data
Lomas Garza, Carmen.
   Making magic windows : creating papel picado/cut-paper art with Carmen Lomas Garza / Carmen Lomas Garza.
      p. cm.
      Summary: Provides instructions for making paper banners and more intricate cut-outs. Includes diagrams for creating specific images.
      ISBN 0-89239-159-6 (pbk.)
      1. Paper work—Juvenile literature.   [1. Paper work. 2. Handicraft.] I. Title
TT870.L65 1999
736'.98—dc21   9838518   CIP   AC

Printed in Korea through Marwin Productions
10   9   8   7   6   5   4   3   2

CONTENTS

INTRODUCTION

For two decades, I have given workshops teaching people of all ages, from young children to adults, how to make *papel picado*, the name for traditional Mexican cut-paper art. This book shows you how to create papel picado with scissors and tissue paper—the same method I use in my workshops. I also tell you how to make cut-paper art with a craft knife.

My experiences with paper cutouts go back to my childhood, when I watched my grandmother cut paper patterns for embroidery designs. From her, I learned how to fold the paper, how to safely hold scissors, and how to cut flowers and geometric shapes. I helped my mother cut paper patterns for decorating cakes and for sewing projects. My father, a professional

sheet-metal worker, cut patterns in aluminum and stainless steel that gave me inspiration for my papel picado.

I have also been influenced by the long history of paper cutouts in Mexico. As early as pre-Columbian times, priests wore elaborate outfits of painted and cut paper representing various gods and the cosmos. Large paper banners adorned buildings and served as flags carried by warriors. Today, papel picado banners, called *banderitas*, are still hung in the plazas of Mexican towns. Mexican artists who mass-produce papel picado have a hammer and special chisels with distinctive points that cut through many layers of tissue paper. Using household scissors and folded tissue paper, people who are not artists make the type of banderitas shown in this book for celebrations such as Christmas or for special occasions such as Día de los Muertos (Day of the Dead). On this national holiday, held on November 2, the dead are granted celestial permission to visit friends and relatives on earth. Colorful paper cutouts—such as dancing or drinking skeletons—are placed at altars to welcome the dead with both respect and humor.

Cut-paper art has a long history in other cultures throughout the world. The Chinese made paper cutouts for use as embroidery designs and also displayed paper cutouts of auspicious symbols. The Japanese created cut-paper stencils for printing designs on fabric. In France before the invention of photography, cut-paper silhouettes were commissioned by people unable to afford an oil portrait.

This book introduces you to the art of papel picado as influenced by Mexican traditions. The projects in the first section use scissors, tissue paper, and folding and cutting techniques that can be followed by people of all ages and accomplished in one session. The cut-paper art created with a craft knife, in the second section, is equally beautiful and rewarding, but takes more time and practice and is best done by adults and by children aged thirteen and older.

Making papel picado is even more enjoyable when many people participate. When people I know are having a birthday or celebrating an anniversary, my gift is to show them and their friends how to make papel picado. After we finish the cutouts, we hang them in a room or outdoors. The bright colors and beautiful designs instantly create a party mood.

When you feel comfortable making some of the projects in this book, I encourage you to experiment with your own designs. The best thing about papel picado is that you can create beautiful cut-paper art even if you aren't a trained artist.

—*Carmen Lomas Garza*

GETTING STARTED WITH PAPEL PICADO

TOOLS AND MATERIALS

small or medium scissors

sheets of tissue paper in white
and assorted colors

string

glue stick

trash bag or waste basket

Y ou want to begin by gathering or purchasing all the tools and materials and arranging them on a work surface. Each person making papel picado art needs a minimum tabletop space of 24 by 24 inches.

The scissors should be sharp and fit comfortably in your hand, allowing you to cut easily and precisely through several layers of tissue paper. I prefer the sharp scissors used to cut for embroidery. Left-handers should use scissors designed to be held in the left hand rather than attempt to cut with scissors for right-handers. You may want to give small children scissors with blunt points.

Tissue paper, found in stationery, art-supply, and craft stores, is commonly sold in packages of sheets measuring approximately 26 by 20 inches. These large sheets can be cut in half to measure 13 by 20 inches. Also available are sheets about 30 by 20 inches, which can be cut in half to 15 by 20 inches. After you feel comfortable working with these half sheets, you may want to use the sheets full size. For your first papel picado projects, it's good to use white tissue paper, which is less expensive than colored tissue. Tissue paper bleeds and disintegrates when wet, so remove all liquids from your work table before you begin.

Be sure to have a trash receptacle on hand for cleaning scraps from your work surface and floor. Cutting out shapes in paper generates many small pieces that you'll want to throw out so they don't get in your way.

When you finish several projects, you can hang them (see page 48), using string held in place with glue. All of the projects begin by making what I call a "string fold" at the top of the paper to hold the string.

HOLDING PAPER AND SCISSORS

The best way to cut paper is to rotate the paper more than you rotate the scissors. Before you begin your first project, try holding the paper and scissors as shown below. Place the paper between the index and middle finger of one hand. I learned from a Chinese master cutter that it's important to sit up straight and hold both paper and scissors at face level. This position allows you to achieve the greatest hand and arm movement. To rotate the paper, simply move the arm and hand holding the paper.

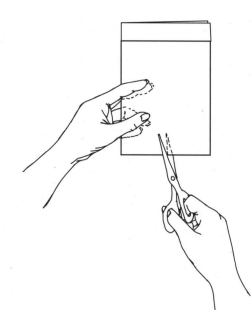

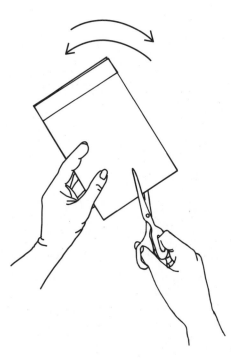

Practicing and Experimenting

Before you make the projects in this book, practice cutting a sheet of white tissue paper or a piece of scrap paper folded once. Try cutting notches like the ones shown here. Then cut curved shapes.

Always leave some space between shapes. Don't worry about creating a particular pattern. After doing several cutouts, you'll notice that you have a distinct style of cutting. When you feel comfortable with the position of your hands, start your first project.

![diagram of paper with cut shapes labeled notch, space, curve, space]

notch *space* *curve* *space*

For each project, you may prefer to begin by following the folding instructions and cutting your own simple shapes. Then, you can cut the specific designs illustrated for each fold. As you'll discover, each folding method can be cut in many ways to yield a wide variety of designs.

After trying the papel picado projects in this book, you can experiment with other ways to fold the paper. Always remember to start by making the string fold so you can later hang the cutouts. And always pay attention to the side edges of the paper so you don't cut them accidentally.

Scissors Safety

At the beginning of my workshops, I always review guidelines for handling scissors safely. It's good to do this at the start, when everyone feels fresh and attentive.

- Never point the scissors at another person.

- Do not hold the scissors in your hand when you touch your face; if you want to scratch your nose, for example, or push your hair away from your face, first put the scissors on the table.

- Do not put the scissors at the edge of the table, where they can accidentally be brushed onto your lap or foot.

- Never twirl the scissors on your finger; they could easily fly off your hand and hurt you or someone else.

Four Cardinal Points

I like to start my workshops with the Four Cardinal Points because it is an easy way to begin working with papel picado art. When you hold up the finished cutout, you'll see a design that reminds you of the north-south and east-west points of a compass. The first two steps of the instructions create a fold that will hold string for hanging several cutouts together (see page 48). I call this the "string fold" and always make it first when I start a project.

1 To make the string fold, fold up about 1 inch at the bottom of the paper.

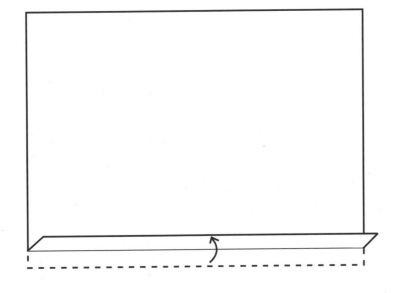

2 Rotate the paper so the string fold is at the top. Remember to keep the string fold at the top and make sure you can always see it—you don't want to cut it accidentally with your scissors. The cutout will be much stronger if the string fold is not cut.

string fold

top

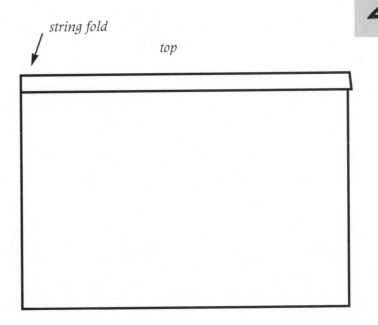

3 Fold the paper back in half, keeping the string fold on the outside of the paper. You don't need to match the corners. Just make sure that the side edges are even.

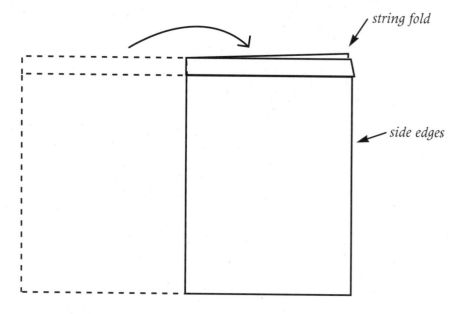

string fold

side edges

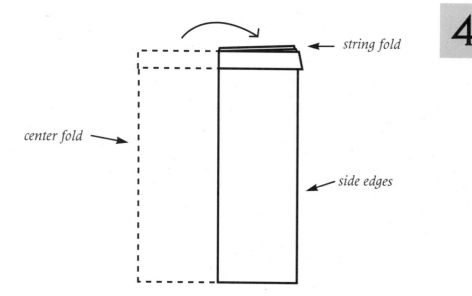

string fold

center fold

side edges

4 Fold the paper back in half again, placing the center fold along the side edges.

5 Fold the paper in half horizontally by bringing the bottom edge up to the string fold. You don't want to cover the flap of the string fold.

string fold

bottom edge

6 Cut the shapes shown along edge *a* and edge *b*. Do not cut shapes in the side edges or the string fold, and do not cut off corner *c*.

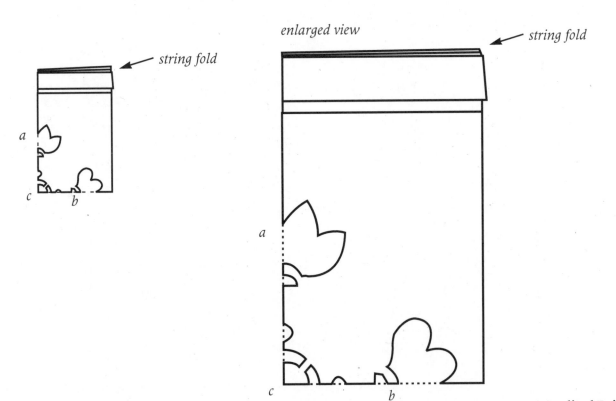

string fold

enlarged view

string fold

a

c   *b*

a

c   *b*

7 Carefully unfold the paper by reversing the folds to step 4. You can now make the cutout more interesting by trimming the bottom to complement your Four Cardinal Points design. Cut the shapes shown here along the bottom edge and right corner.

For this project—and as a final step for some of the other projects in this book—you can trim the bottom using the stair steps, scallops, points, wavy line, or fringe shown below. You can even simply cut an angle.

When you have trimmed the bottom, carefully open the cutout by reversing the folds.

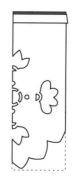

enlarged view

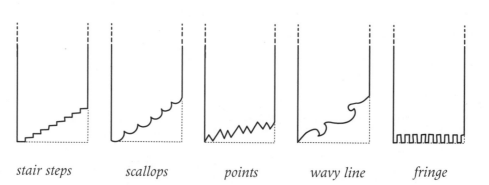

stair steps   *scallops*   *points*   *wavy line*   *fringe*

TWINKLING
STARS

My name for this papel picado project is Twinkling Stars, but the design you create might remind you of eight-petaled flowers. It is easy to make this right after the Four Cardinal Points because it repeats the first five steps of that project.

1 To make the string fold, fold up about 1 inch at the bottom of the paper.

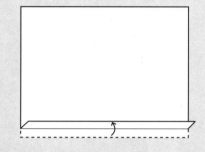

2 Rotate the paper so the string fold is at the top. Remember to keep the string fold at the top and make sure you can always see it—you don't want to cut it accidentally with your scissors. The cutout will be much stronger if the string fold is not cut.

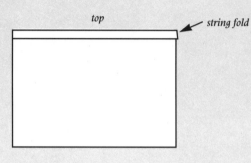

top string fold

3 Fold the paper back in half, keeping the string fold on the outside of the paper. You don't need to match the corners. Just make sure that the side edges are even.

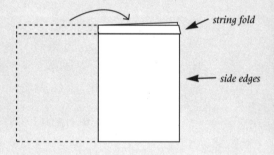

string fold

side edges

4 Fold the paper back in half again, placing the center fold along the side edges.

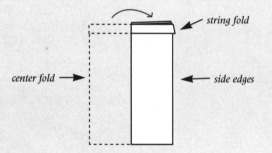

string fold

center fold → ← side edges

5 Fold the paper in half horizontally by bringing the bottom edge up to the string fold. You don't want to cover the flap of the string fold.

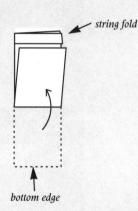

string fold

bottom edge

6 Fold the paper at an angle by placing the bottom folded edge along edge *a*.

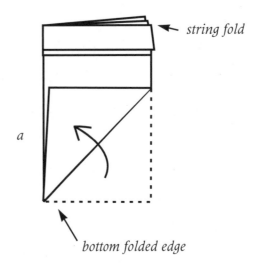

string fold

a

bottom folded edge

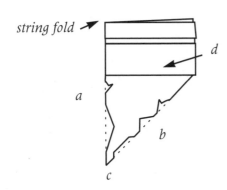

string fold

d

a

b

c

7 Cut the shapes shown along edge *a* and edge *b*. Do not cut corner *c* or cut above fold *d*. Remember not to cut shapes in the string fold.

enlarged view

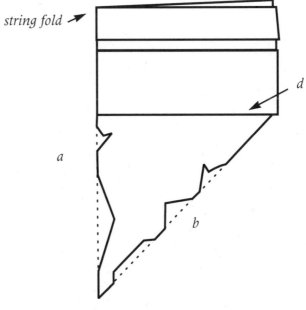

string fold

d

a

b

c

8 Carefully unfold the paper by reversing the folds to step 4. You can now make the cutout more interesting by trimming the bottom to complement your Twinkling Stars design. Cut the shapes shown here along the bottom edge. Carefully open the cutout by reversing the folds.

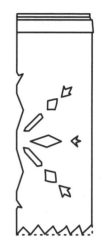

bottom edge

enlarged view

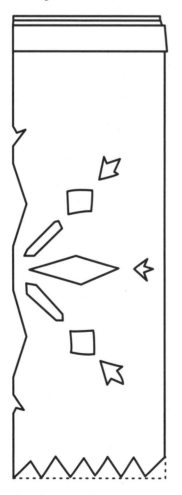

bottom edge

FLOWERS

Two big, joyful flowers bloom in this papel picado project. To begin making these flowers, you follow the first six steps of Twinkling Stars.

1 To make the string fold, fold up about 1 inch at the bottom of the paper.

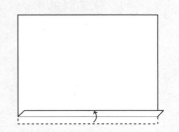

2 Rotate the paper so the string fold is at the top. Remember to keep the string fold at the top and make sure you can always see it—you don't want to cut it accidentally with your scissors. The cutout will be much stronger if the string fold is not cut.

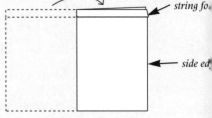

3 Fold the paper back in half, keeping the string fold on the outside of the paper. You don't need to match the corners. Just make sure that the side edges are even.

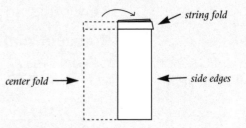

4 Fold the paper back in half again, placing the center fold along the side edges.

5 Fold the paper in half horizontally by bringing the bottom edge up to the string fold. You don't want to cover the flap of the string fold.

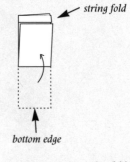

6 Fold the paper at an angle by placing the bottom edge along edge *a*.

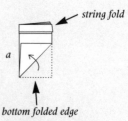

7 Fold edge *b* back so that it is even with edge *a*. The side edges and part of the string fold will peek out at the top.

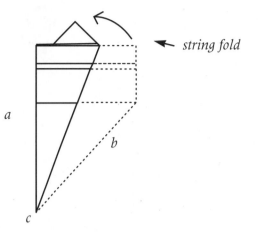

string fold

a

b

c

8 Cut the shapes shown along edge *a/b* and edge *d*. Do not cut off corner *c* or cut above edge *e*. Remember not to cut the string fold.

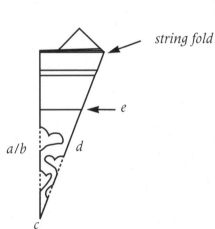

string fold

e

a/b *d*

c

enlarged view

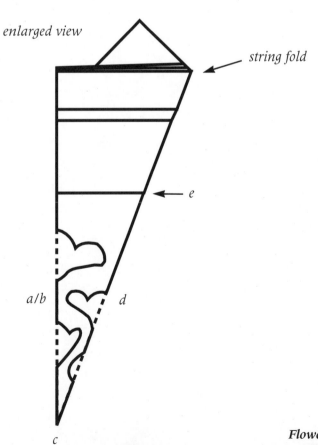

string fold

e

a/b *d*

c

Carefully unfold the paper by reversing the folds to step
4. You can now make the cutout more interesting by
trimming the bottom to complement your Flowers
design. Cut the shapes shown here along the bottom edge
and right corner. Carefully open the cutout by reversing
the folds.

bottom edge

enlarged view

bottom edge

FLOWERS WITH LEAVES

Making this papel picado lets you combine flowers and leaves. You begin by repeating the first eight steps of Flowers, but you cut different shapes for the petals. Then you unfold and refold the paper and cut the leaves.

To make the string fold, fold up about 1 inch at the bottom of the paper.

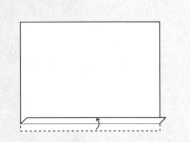

 Rotate the paper so the string fold is at the top. Remember to keep the string fold at the top and make sure you can always see it—you don't want to cut it accidentally with your scissors. The cutout will be much stronger if the string fold is not cut.

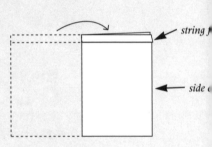 Fold the paper back in half, keeping the string fold on the outside of the paper. You don't need to match the corners. Just make sure that the side edges are even.

 Fold the paper back in half again, placing the center fold along the side edges.

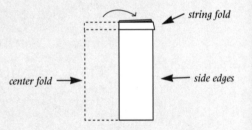

 Fold the paper in half horizontally by bringing the bottom edge up to the string fold. You don't want to cover the flap of the string fold.

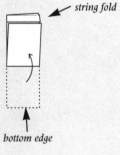

 Fold the paper at an angle by placing the bottom edge along edge *a*.

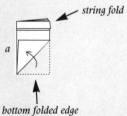

7 Fold edge *b* back so that it is even with edge *a*. The side edges and part of the string fold will peek out at the top.

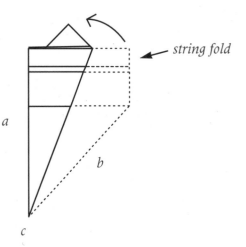

string fold

a

b

c

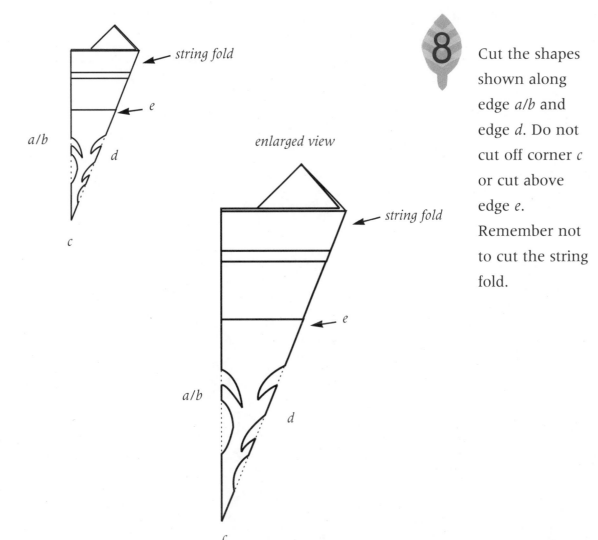

string fold

e

a/b

d

c

enlarged view

string fold

e

a/b

d

c

8 Cut the shapes shown along edge *a/b* and edge *d*. Do not cut off corner *c* or cut above edge *e*. Remember not to cut the string fold.

9 Carefully unfold the paper by reversing the folds to step 5.

enlarged view

 10 Fold the paper at an angle by bringing the right edge up so it is parallel to, but not touching or on top of, the flap of the string fold.

enlarged view

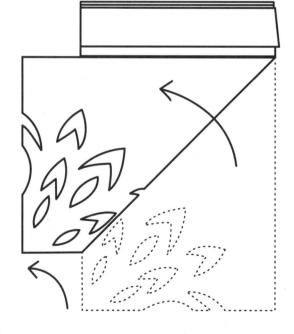

11 Cut the leaf shapes shown in edge *f*.

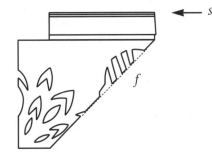

enlarged view

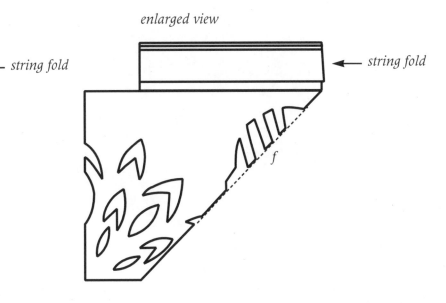

← *string fold*

← *string fold*

f

f

12 Carefully unfold the paper by reversing the folds to step 4. You can now make the cutout more interesting by trimming the bottom to complement your Flowers with Leaves. Cut the shapes shown here along the bottom edge. Carefully open the cutout by reversing the folds.

enlarged view

bottom edge

bottom edge

DIAMONDS

This project has lots of diamonds, both big and small. When you unfold the finished papel picado, you'll see two big diamonds—each made of much smaller diamonds.

1   To make the string fold, fold up about 1 inch at the bottom of the paper.

2   Rotate the paper so the string fold is at the top. Remember to keep the string fold at the top and make sure you can always see it—you don't want to cut it accidentally with your scissors. The cutout will be much stronger if the string fold is not cut.

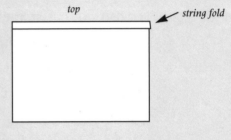

3   Fold the paper back in half, keeping the string fold on the outside of the paper. You don't need to match the corners. Just make sure that the side edges are even.

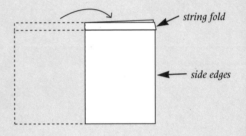

4   Fold the paper back in half again, placing the center fold along the side edges.

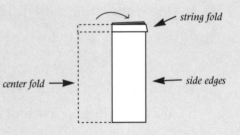

5   Fold the paper in half horizontally by bringing the bottom edge up to the string fold. You don't want to cover the flap of the string fold.

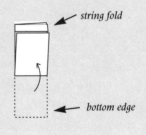

6   Fold the paper at an angle by placing the bottom edge along edge *a*.

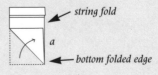

7 Cut the shapes shown in edge *b*. Do not cut off corner *c* or cut above fold *d*. Do not cut shapes in edge *a*—these are the side edges of the cutout—and remember not to cut shapes in the string fold.

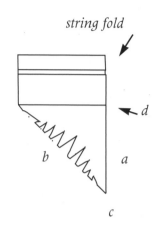

string fold

← *d*

b

a

c

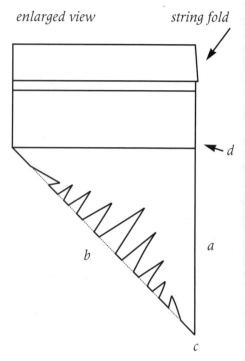

enlarged view   *string fold*

← *d*

b

a

c

8 Carefully unfold the paper by reversing the folds to step 4. You can now make the cutout more interesting by trimming the bottom to complement your Diamonds design. Cut as shown here along the bottom edge. Carefully open the cutout by reversing the folds.

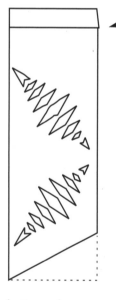

← *string fold*

bottom edge

enlarged view

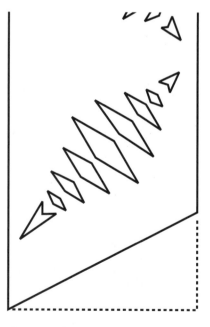

bottom edge

TILES

The rows of shapes in this papel picado make me think of the colorful hand-painted tiles that decorate many Mexican buildings. Only one cutting step is needed to create the tiles. Because the paper is folded step by step into an ever smaller "package," the tiles are repeated across the paper.

1   To make the string fold, fold up about 1 inch at the bottom of the paper.

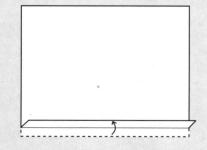

2   Rotate the paper so the string fold is at the top. Remember to keep the string fold at the top and make sure you can always see it—you don't want to cut it accidentally with your scissors. The cutout will be much stronger if the string fold is not cut.

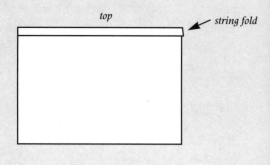

3   Fold the paper back in half, keeping the string fold on the outside of the paper. You don't need to match the corners. Just make sure that the side edges are even.

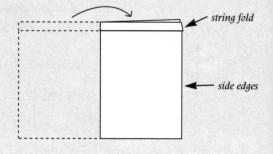

4   Fold the paper back in half again, placing the center fold along the side edges.

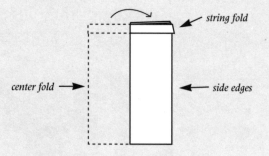

5   Fold the paper in half horizontally by bringing the bottom edge up to the string fold. You don't want to cover the flap of the string fold.

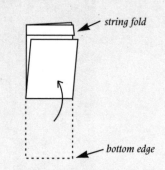

6 Again fold the paper back in half. Remember to keep the side edges even.

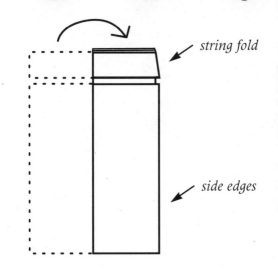

string fold

side edges

7 Again fold the paper in half horizontally by bringing the bottom edge up to the string fold. Remember that you don't want to cover the flap of the string fold.

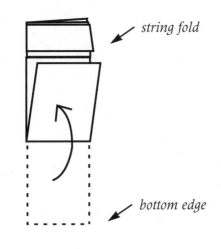

string fold

bottom edge

string fold

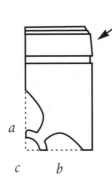

a

c   b

enlarged view

string fold

a

c   b

8 Cut the shape shown along edge *a* and the other shape shown along edge *b*. This is the one time when you want to cut off corner *c*, as shown.

9 Carefully unfold the paper by reversing the folds to step 4. You can now make the cutout more interesting by trimming the bottom to complement your Tiles design. Cut the shapes shown here along the bottom edge. Carefully open the cutout by reversing the folds.

string fold

bottom edge

enlarged view

bottom edge

THE FAN

This is one of my favorite projects because the shapes radiate from a central point, and the cutout is so graceful when hung. I also like it because it has many images—leaves, hummingbirds, flowers. When you first make the Fan, don't worry if the shapes that you cut don't look like my shapes. You'll still have a graceful fan shape with a beautiful design. With some practice, you'll soon be able to make leaves, flowers, and hummingbirds.

1 To make the string fold, fold up about 1 inch at the bottom of the paper.

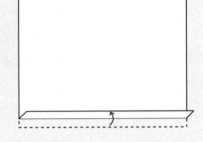

2 Rotate the paper so the string fold is at the top. Remember to keep the string fold at the top and make sure you can always see it—you don't want to cut it accidentally with your scissors. The cutout will be much stronger if the string fold is not cut.

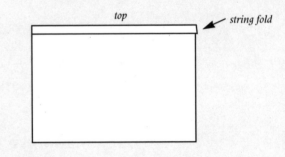

top

string fold

3 Fold the paper back in half, keeping the string fold on the outside of the paper. You don't need to match the corners. Just make sure that the side edges are even.

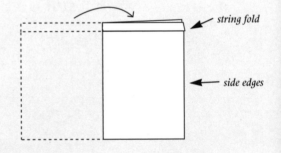

string fold

side edges

4 Hold your left index finger just below the string fold at point *x*. With your right hand, lift up the lower left corner of the paper and fold it at an angle so that the center fold (*cf*) is parallel to, but not touching or on top of, the flap of the string fold.

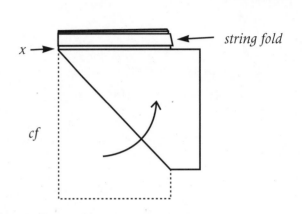

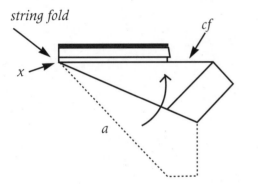

5 Again hold your left index finger at point *x*. This time, take the lower right corner of the paper and fold it at an angle by placing edge *a* on top of the center fold (*cf*). Edge *a* should be parallel to, but not touching or on top of, the flap of the string fold.

6 Fold the paper one more time at an angle—by placing edge *b* on top of edge *a* and the center fold (*cf*). Like the other edges, this one should be parallel to, but not touching or on top of, the flap of the string fold. The layers of folded paper will resemble a necktie on its side.

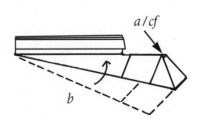

7 Cut the end of this "necktie" as shown at any point beyond the string fold.

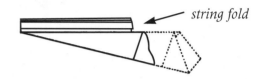
string fold

enlarged view

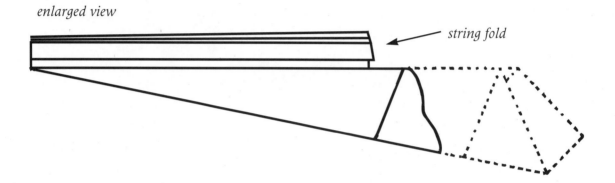
string fold

8 Cut the shapes shown along edge *c*, beginning at the end closest to point *x*. At this end there is very little space, so the first shapes will have to be small. But as you cut along the edge, you will have more space to cut larger shapes. Make sure that you do not cut beyond folds *a/cf/b* or beyond the side edges.

string fold

x

c

enlarged view

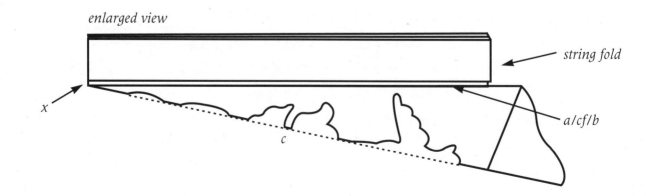
string fold

x

c

a/cf/b

9 Unfold once to bring down all the edges (*a/cf/b*), then cut the shapes shown in edge *d*. Carefully open the cutout by reversing the folds.

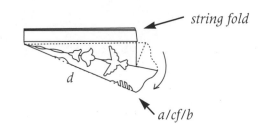

enlarged view

THE ZIGZAG

Where I grew up in Texas, I always saw lizards when I went outside. Remembering how the angles of their legs are like zigzags, I made the lizards part of this papel picado filled with zigzag designs.

To make the string fold, fold up about 1 inch at the bottom of the paper.

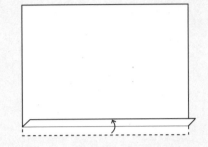

Rotate the paper so the string fold is at the top. Remember to keep the string fold at the top and make sure you can always see it—you don't want to cut it accidentally with your scissors. The cutout will be much stronger if the string fold is not cut.

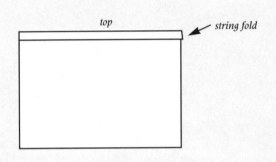

Fold the paper back in half, keeping the string fold on the outside of the paper. You don't need to match the corners. Just make sure that the side edges are even.

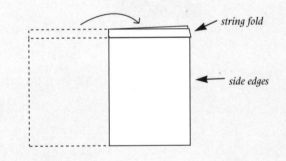

 Place the paper on the table and rotate it so that the string fold is on your left and the center fold (*cf*) is right in front of you. It is very important to leave the paper on the table to make the rest of the folds.

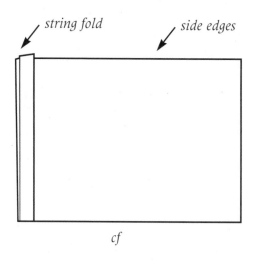

string fold　*side edges*

cf

 **5** Fold the paper horizontally by bringing the center fold (*cf*) up to about ¼ inch away from the side edges. This ¼-inch space will allow you to see the side edges at all times so you won't accidentally cut shapes in them.

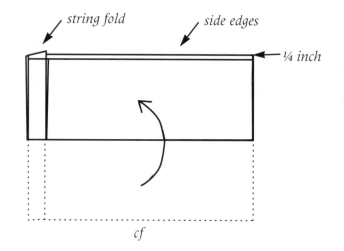

string fold　*side edges*

¼ inch

cf

6 Fold the paper again—by bringing edge *a* directly on top of the center fold (*cf*). Be sure to leave ¼ inch between edge *a* and the side edges.

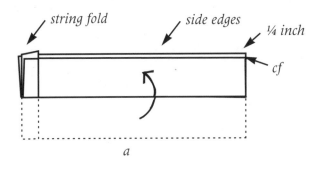

string fold   side edges   ¼ inch   cf

a

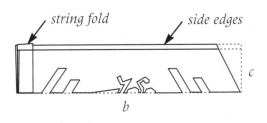

string fold   side edges

c

b

7 Cut the shapes shown along edges *b* and *c*. Remember not to cut the string fold or the side edges.

enlarged view

string fold   side edges

c

b

Unfold once to bring all of the edges (*cf/a/b*) away from the side edges. Cut the shapes shown along edge *e*. Carefully open the cutout by reversing the folds.

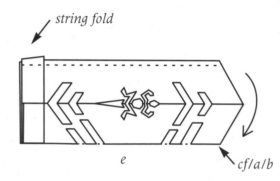

string fold

e

cf/a/b

enlarged view

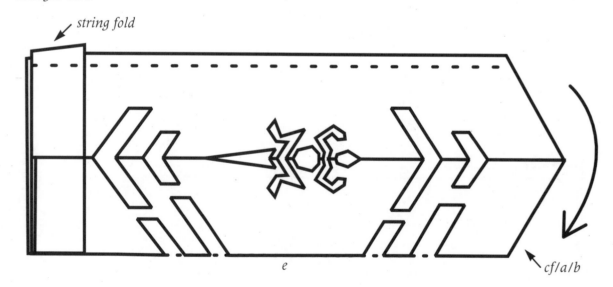

string fold

e

cf/a/b

HANGING YOUR PAPEL PICADO ART

Any room or backyard is festive when decorated with papel picado. I think that the cutouts look best when hung across the room rather than placed directly on the wall. This way, you can walk under them and see them flutter in the slightest breeze.

Measuring your room and hanging the cutouts is easier and goes faster when two people work together.

1. Use string to measure across the room. Make a knot where the string touches each wall, and leave an extra 2 feet of string at each end, beyond the knot to facilitate hanging.

2. Stack the cutouts in the order of colors and designs you want. I feel it's best not to have two of the same color and preferably not of the same design next to one another. All of the projects except the Fan and the Zigzag can be cut in half through the center fold to make two smaller cutouts. When hanging the "halves," string them in multiples of two, so the cutouts stack neatly, accordion style, for storage.

3. Place the first cutout you want to hang on the table. Arrange it so the string fold is closest to you and facing up. Open the string fold, and run a glue stick down the length of the crease and the flap. Set the string in the crease. Remember to place the knot in

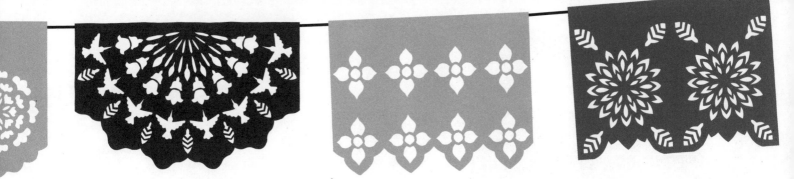

the string beyond the edge of the cutout, as shown here. Fold down the flap and press to seal the string in the fold. The glue not only seals the flap but keeps the cutouts in place on the string.

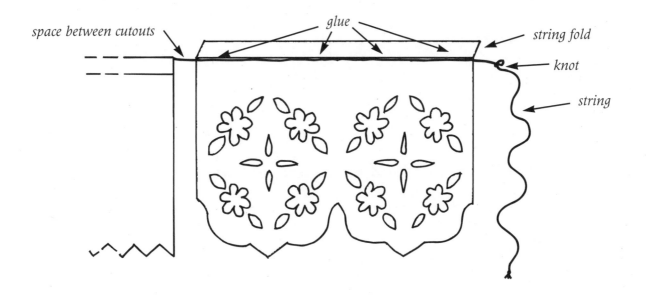

space between cutouts

glue

string fold

knot

string

4. Repeat the process until you reach the second knot in the string. Be sure to leave 1 to 2 inches between cutouts.

5. The assembled cutouts are light enough that you can attach the string to the walls with pushpins. Hang them high enough so there's enough space for everyone to walk underneath.

Making Papel Picado with a Craft Knife

TOOLS AND MATERIALS

drawing paper in various sizes and colors, including black

white and colored typing paper

craft knife such as X-ACTO number 1 with safety anti-roll cap

triangular anti-roll tube (if your knife does not have an anti-roll cap)

number 11 blades for a craft knife

lead pencil and eraser

white or yellow colored pencil

plastic cutting board

ruler

Sunburst pattern (see page 59)

optional: X-ACTO Professional Swivel Knife number X3051

Making papel picado with a craft knife requires more cutting and drawing skills, and therefore more time, than cutting papel picado with scissors. As you can see by the list here, craft-knife projects also call for more tools and materials. Some, like the pencil, eraser, and ruler, are items you probably have on hand. For other items, like the craft knife and plastic cutting board, you'll need to make a trip to an art-supply or craft store. Keep in mind that a craft knife is not an appropriate tool for young children. But with preparation and guidance, children age thirteen and up are able to handle a knife safely and enjoy creating these cutouts.

Rather than cutting thin tissue paper as for the scissor projects, you will use drawing paper. Paper in various sizes and many colors is sold at art-supply and craft stores. Most sheets are rectangular, so you'll need to cut them into squares for the Sunburst project in this book. When you practice handling a craft knife, you'll want to use typing paper, which is less expensive than drawing paper.

When you buy a craft knife, make sure that you purchase an extra supply of blades. If you already own a craft knife, check that it has a safety anti-roll cap. If it doesn't, add a triangular anti-roll tube to your shopping list. A plastic cutting board will protect your work surface, help keep the craft-knife blades sharp, and make cutting easier and faster. These boards come in a range of sizes.

The optional swivel knife is more expensive than a craft knife like the X-ACTO number 1. This knife is not required for making the Sunburst, but advanced cutters may prefer it and will find it handy later for cutting their own papel picado designs.

CRAFT-KNIFE SAFETY

Cutouts made with a craft knife are intricate
and beautiful. But the very tool that makes this kind
of papel picado so appealing can also be dangerous. Every time
you're about to start working, review these safety guidelines to
avoid accidents.

• Always use the knife on a cutting board. The board both protects your
  work surface and helps you cut easily and safely.

• Hold the knife the way you hold a pencil—but do not rest your index
  finger on the back of the blade. Keep your finger on the knife handle at
  all times.

• Place your other hand on the paper opposite the direction you are
  cutting, as shown here. You will have greater control of the knife if you
  pull it toward you when you are cutting than if you push it away from
  you. Use the hand holding the paper—not the hand holding the knife—to
  rotate the paper together with the cutting board so you are always cutting
  comfortably toward you.

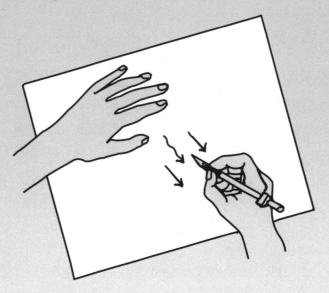

- Give yourself safety reminders. As soon as you place the knife on the paper with one hand, ask yourself, "Where is my other hand? Is it in a safe position?" Accidents are more apt to happen when your attention wanders and you're not observing the safe hand positions shown opposite.

- When you're not using the knife, place it in the center of the table. Make sure that the anti-roll cap is on the knife or insert a triangular anti-roll tube. A knife that rolls off the table can easily stab your leg or foot, or someone else's.

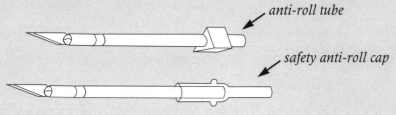

anti-roll tube

safety anti-roll cap

- Cutting paper with your craft knife is safer when you begin with a new sharp blade. A dull blade takes more effort to use.

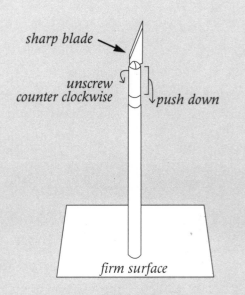

sharp blade

unscrew counter clockwise

push down

firm surface

To replace the blade, hold the knife, end down, in a standing position on a firm surface, as shown here. Unscrew the blade holder in a counter clockwise direction. Push down on the blade holder to loosen the blade grip. Carefully lift out the old blade and discard properly. Then insert a new blade and tighten the blade holder by screwing it in a clockwise direction.

CRAFT-KNIFE CUTTING TECHNIQUES

cross the cut

cross the cut

cross the cut

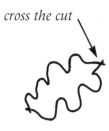

cross the cut

Before you start the Sunburst cutout, practice cutting plain typing or writing paper placed on your plastic cutting board. At this point, don't draw on the paper or try to cut a particular design. Instead, you want to get comfortable holding the knife and paper safely, as shown in "Craft-Knife Safety." Practicing also helps you warm up your hand and arm muscles.

Start by cutting large shapes, then gradually cut smaller and smaller shapes. Try cutting curved shapes and also shapes with straight edges and angles. When you connect the curved or straight cuts of a shape, cross the cuts at the corners, as shown here, so that the cutout pieces of paper can easily be removed. If the pieces are still attached, you'll be tempted to tear them from the paper. This will leave unattractive rips and burrs in your design.

As you practice, check that the knife blade is sharp, and replace it if it is dull. Remember to check the location of your hands and adjust them if necessary so they are in the safest position.

Advanced cutters working with the Professional Swivel Knife will also want to practice. With this knife, you can cut out small shapes by pulling or pushing the knife in any direction. You can also cut very tight curves. The key to using this knife effectively is to always hold it perfectly perpendicular to the paper so the blade can swivel in any direction.

Essential Elements of Design

It's important to understand two aspects of creating papel picado with a craft knife: the use of positive and negative areas and the function of connectors.

When making a craft-knife cutout, you cut away shapes with your knife. These shapes are called the negative areas of the design. The resulting paper cutout is the positive area of the design.

There are three types of designs. I call them silhouette, stencil, and outline. As you develop your design skills, you can combine all three types within one cutout.

silhouette   *stencil*   *outline*

The silhouette and the outline do not need a border. But designs that are enclosed in a border are more durable and can be hung directly on a wall or over a window without being framed first. If you want to make a borderless, or freestanding, cutout like those below, you can sandwich it between two sheets of picture glass, using simple framing hardware. When hung on the wall, the cutout seems to float away from the wall.

silhouette   *outline*

Connectors are positive areas of the design that hold the cutout together. There are two types of connectors. In the most intriguing cutouts, the way that the subject is cut out provides the needed connectors without calling attention to their function. In other words, the subject acts as its own connectors. In the cutout shown at right, the flower petals, as well as the leaf and tendril, are connected to the border.

connector →   *← connecto*

← connec

The other form of connector is a grid, like the one in the work below, which connects the subject to the border. The design for this connector needs to be drawn on the paper before the paper is cut. First, the subject of the cutout is drawn on the paper, then a ruler is used to measure and draw the grid lines.

Carmen Lomas Garza shows an example of her papel picado art with grid connectors.

■ DESIGN TIP

Make a habit of drawing on the back of the paper. Once the paper is cut, it is difficult to erase the pencil lines. If you design your own cutouts and want to use letters, remember to draw the letters backward so that they read correctly on the front of the finished cutout. On light-colored papers, use a regular pencil. On black and other dark-colored papers, use a white or yellow colored pencil.

SUNBURST

This simple design introduces you to the importance of connectors and positive and negative areas of a craft-knife cutout. Here, the subject provides its own connectors—the rays emanating from the sun secure it to the border. I suggest using yellow paper—but you can use another color or you can make several suns in a variety of colors. To make more than one Sunburst, simply trace the template you just used on a clean sheet of paper to create a new template.

Make a photocopy of the Sunburst pattern on page 59. When you copy the pattern, enlarge it proportionally to fit the square sheet of drawing paper you have chosen for the project.

 Fold the square sheet of paper in half. Use a ruler to draw a border of at least 1 inch around the outside edge of the paper.

 Place the pattern on the center fold. To hold the pattern in place, staple it to the paper in two negative areas that will be cut out last, next to the border.

 If the rays of the sun on the pattern do not reach the border, you can extend them with a pencil until they connect with the border. If you make a line that you do not need, erase it so that you will not later cut on the line by mistake.

 Cut out the white portions of the pattern by starting with the smallest areas. Remember to cross the cuts at the corners so you can easily remove the cutout pieces of paper.

 Open the finished cutout. You can flatten the cutout by sandwiching it between two sheets of same-sized paper and placing it on a flat surface underneath a stack of books. You can also sandwich the cutout between two sheets of plain tissue paper and press it with a barely warm iron (on the "silk" setting).

SUNBURST PATTERN

staple

center fold

staple

MULTIPLE TISSUE PAPER CUTOUTS

The artists of Mexico who mass-produce cutouts use a hammer and special chisels to cut through many layers of tissue paper. To make multiple copies of a cutout, you can use a craft knife. For durable cutouts that will last for months outdoors, use solid-color plastic sheets cut from recycled plastic bags or plastic table covers. Stack and cut the sheets as directed below; when hanging them on string, choose a glue suitable for plastic.

1 Begin by making a master drawing, or pattern, of your design. The drawing should be on paper that is the same weight as typing or writing paper and is the same size as the sheets of tissue paper you will use. Allow enough space at the top of your drawing for a string fold.

2 Stack no more than 15 sheets of tissue paper. Place the master drawing on top and staple it to the stack of tissue paper in two or three negative areas near the border and in two positive areas on the border.

3 Using the craft knife, cut out the negative portions of your design, starting with the smallest areas. You'll need to cross the cuts at the corners a little more than you did for the Sunburst, to make sure that the bottom layers of tissue paper are cut and the pieces of paper can easily be removed.

4 Carefully remove the staples in the border and separate the cutouts. To make additional cutouts of the same design, trace the drawing you just used on a clean sheet of paper and repeat the stacking and cutting. Hang the cutouts by following the directions on pages 48–49.

ABOUT THE AUTHOR

Carmen Lomas Garza is one of the foremost Mexican American painters and printmakers. In her most recent book for children, *Magic Windows/Ventanas mágicas*—a companion to this workbook—she uses the traditional art form of papel picado to tell stories about her family and community. Two of her previous books, *Family Pictures/Cuadros de familia* and *In My Family/En mi familia*, have received many prestigious awards, including the Pura Belpré Honor Award from the American Library Association, the Tomas Rivera Children's Book Award, and the Américas Award.

Carmen has exhibited her paintings, prints, and papel picado in major galleries and museums. She has also created large-scale steel and copper works based on her papel picado cutouts, one of which is on display at the San Francisco International Airport. Carmen currently lives in San Francisco, California.